YOUR KNOWLEDGE HAS VALUE

- We will publish your bachelor's and master's thesis, essays and papers

- Your own eBook and book - sold worldwide in all relevant shops

- Earn money with each sale

Upload your text at www.GRIN.com
and publish for free

Burberry's Digital Transformation. Evolution, Challenges, and Future Directions

Bibliographic information published by the German National Library:

The German National Library lists this publication in the National Bibliography; detailed bibliographic data are available on the Internet at http://dnb.dnb.de.

ISBN: 9783389094990
This book is also available as an ebook.

© GRIN Publishing GmbH
Trappentreustraße 1
80339 München

Print and binding: Books on Demand GmbH, Norderstedt, Germany
Printed on acid-free paper from responsible sources.

The present work has been carefully prepared. Nevertheless, authors and publishers do not incur liability for the correctness of information, notes, links and advice as well as any printing errors.

GRIN web shop: https://www.grin.com/document/1523038

Digital transformation at Burberry

Akademie für Mode & Design
Mode & Designmanagement
WS 2023/24
3. Semester
Digital Transformation
Abgabedatum: 26.01.2023

Table of contents

1. Introduction

In the contemporary dynamic technological landscape, businesses must undergo digital transformation to sustain competitiveness. The business realm has experienced a swift evolution in recent years, marked by the widespread adoption of new technologies by companies aiming to enhance operational efficiency and optimize financial performance.

Even well-established brands, such as Burberry, must adapt to digital transformation to remain relevant, maintain and to improve their brand image. Burberry, founded in 1856, has experienced both successes and setbacks. However, in the last two decades, the brand has re-established itself as a prominent luxury brand, largely due to its digital transformation and rebranding efforts.

This assignment examines Burberry's evolution through digital transformation, including the strategic initiatives and technological advancements employed by the luxury fashion brand to maintain a leading position in the ever-changing retail environment. It also considers the challenges the brand faces during this transformation. The focus is on the seamless incorporation of digital features in physical stores. Burberry's response to the challenges presented by the digital era is showcased as an impactful case study, achieved by harnessing the power of mobile technology and online platforms. The assignment will align a digital transformation type with Burberry and then focus on its future direction. The conclusion reflects on Burberry's digital transformation.

2. The brand Burberry

Founded in 1856 by 21-year-old Thomas Burberry in Basingstoke, Burberry was established with the idea of clothing that would protect the customer from British weather. Almost twenty years later Gabardine was invented. This fabric would revolutionize outdoor wear due to its breathable, light, and waterproof characteristics. Burberry then filed for patent in 1888. In 1893 polar explorer Dr. Fridtjof Nansen wore gabardine fabric by Burberry when he made an excursion to the north pole. Considered the predecessor to the trench coat, the Tielocken coat, designed by Thomas Burberry, which just closes with a single strap, is designed. During the first world war the iconic trench coat is introduced, fitted for the military with D-rings used to carry grenades and gun flaps to provide additional protection when in battle. The famous Burberry check, which is known today, is registered as a trademark in the 1920s. As early as the 1960s every fifth coat exported from Britain is a Burberry product.[1] Over the years, Burberry expanded its product range to include accessories, fragrances, and a wide variety of clothing items. The brand established a strong global presence and became synonymous with British style and luxury. At the start of the 21st century, Burberry had lost its association with the British high society and had become more associated with chav culture. As a result, it was often targeted by cheap imitations.[2]

After Angela Ahrendts became CEO in 2006, Burberry started to become a highly digital brand. She revitalized the underperforming brand, focusing on its heritage while also appealing to a younger and more fashion-forward demographic. Burberry is the first brand to livestream a fashion show online. The Brand took it even further one year later, as the whole collection debuted on Twitter before it was seen on the runway.[3] In 2018, under the creative direction of Riccardo Tisci, Burberry rebranded its iconic check pattern and introduced a new, modern version known as the "Thomas Burberry Monogram." This marked a significant change in the brand's visual identity while still honoring its heritage. Burberry has also made efforts to be more environmentally responsible. They have

---

[1] Vgl. „Burberry: Our History" burberry.com
(https://uk.burberry.com/c/our-history/ letzter Stand: 08.11.2023)
[2] Vgl. Tiwari, Tanu: "Burberry's Jaw-dropping Digital Transformation", linkedin.com, 01.02.2021
(https://www.linkedin.com/pulse/burberrys-jaw-dropping-digital-transformation-tanu-tiwari/ letzter Stand: 10.11.2023)
[3] Vgl. „House History: The Burberry Timeline" hautehistory.co.uk, 28.07.2020
(http://www.hautehistory.co.uk/burberry-timeline/house-history-the-burberry-timeline letzter Stand: 08.11.2023)

introduced initiatives to reduce waste and their carbon footprint and have pledged to become carbon neutral by 2022.[4]

3. Digital transformation

In the current era of VUCA (Volatility, Uncertainty, Complexity, Ambiguity), leaders must ensure their companies can adapt to an ever-changing society. Digital transformation is the driving force behind fundamental change in companies. To excel in agility, efficiency, and customer-centricity, it is essential to undergo digital transformation. This not only adds new value for stakeholders, employees, and customers but also helps achieve these goals objectively.[5]

Digital transformation poses various challenges for companies, spanning across several, diverse domains. Social challenges include resistance due to fear of change, while legal challenges include data and identity theft, hacker attacks, and changes in the work environment due to AI. Furthermore, companies require a greater number of digitally competent experts than ever before. The work of senior employees may be affected by this factor, as they may not be as familiar with digital technology as their younger counterparts, who are more IT-focused.[6]

Digital transformation may involve implementing an online store, enhancing the online store with new features, digitizing physical stores, and exploring novel online marketing strategies, among other possibilities. To incorporate these characteristics, a new business strategy may be necessary, along with a shift in the mindset of company leaders. A new of handling data is also required, as well as a new way of structuring the team.

4. Digital transformation at Burberry

Ever since Angela Ahrendts took over Burberry, the brand has been a digital leader in the fashion world. The brand has undergone a significant digital transformation in recent years

---

[4] Vgl. „Sustainable Development Goals" burberry.com
(https://www.burberryplc.com/impact/Our-Approach/sustainable-development-goals letzter Stand: 08.11.2023)
[5] Vgl. „What is digital transformation?", Accenture.com
(https://www.accenture.com/us-en/insights/digital-transformation-index# letzter Stand: 14.01.2024)
[6] Vgl. Sacolick, Isaac: „Digital transformation challenges and 14 ways to solve them", techtarget.com, 01.11.2023
(https://www.techtarget.com/searchcio/tip/3-biggest-digital-transformation-challenges-and-how-to-solve-them letzter Stand: 14.01.2024)

to adapt to the rapidly changing landscape of the fashion industry and cater to the evolving preferences and behaviors of its customers. With "The Art of the Trench" in 2009, a social network dedicated to the Burberry trench coat, and the first runway show being livestreamed by Burberry, the brand has been coming closer to their goal to be the first fully digital luxury fashion brand.[7] Burberry cut the pandemic-hit, that had hit the luxury market hard, with a well-rounded digital strategy and progressed on digital strategy.[8]

4.1 Burberry's challenges due to digital transformation

Since the Covid-19 pandemic began, the retail industry has undergone significant changes. Economic downturns, reduced customer incomes, and lockdowns have all contributed to changes in consumer behavior. Many customers, particularly younger ones, have turned to online shopping for convenience, resulting in a significant increase in digital sales for brands. The closure of physical stores has led many luxury fashion brands to focus more on online sales, forcing them to reshape their business models and accelerate digital transformation. Online sales in the luxury market have increased, with online purchases accounting for 12% of general sales and 23% in 2020. It is predicted that by 2025, online channels will be the primary source for luxury purchases, driving the need for omnichannel transformation. Burberry efficiently integrates customers through online events. The brand also employs localized and regional content to build digital communities worldwide, as well as personalized products that enhance consumer journeys. Luxury brands must prioritize digitalization to create immersive shopping experiences that meet customer expectations. The luxury goods market has been fundamentally impacted by changes in lifestyle, shopping habits, and values. Due to the Covid-19 pandemic, Burberry's revenue and profits have plummeted during a critical time in its luxury transformation plan. The company's current assets increased by 17.4% from 2020 to 2021, indicating an improvement in its financial position.[9]

---

[7] Vgl. McKinnon, Tricia: "How Burberry is Building the Store of the Future", indigo9digital.com, 03.06.2022
(https://www.indigo9digital.com/blog/burberrysocialretailstoreofthefuture letzter Stand: 10.11.2023)
[8] Vgl. Zhu, Zhengjia: "The Impact of Digital Transformation on the Fashion Industry in the Post-Pandemic Era", researchgate.com, April 2023
(https://www.researchgate.net/publication/370578695_The_Impact_of_Digital_Transformation_on_the_Fashion_Industry_in_the_Post-Pandemic_Era letzter Stand: 27.12.2023)

[9] Vgl. Zhu, Zhengjia: "The Impact of Digital Transformation on the Fashion Industry in the Post-Pandemic Era", researchgate.com, April 2023
(https://www.researchgate.net/publication/370578695_The_Impact_of_Digital_Transformation_on_the_Fashion_Industry_in_the_Post-Pandemic_Era letzter Stand: 27.12.2023)

Burberry's 2021 financial report reveals that the Asia-Pacific region accounts for 52.5% of the company's total turnover, with an annual revenue of £1.2 billion. Any changes in the economic, social, regulatory, and political environment in Asia could significantly impact the company.[10]

4.2 Case study 1: The digital retail store in London

In 2012, Burberry opened a flagship store in London's Regent district, aiming to redefine the intersection of digital and physical shopping experiences. Upon entering the store, customers are enveloped in an environment designed to emulate the brand's website. The store incorporates digital signage screens embedded in floors and enveloping walls, live-streaming hubs, and mirrors. These screens showcase models strutting down catwalks during Burberry shows, adding a dynamic and visually immersive element to the shopping experience. Customers also can use their smartphones to identify items, saving them to their online checkout accounts for later online purchases, even if the products are physically present in the store.

Furthermore, the store employs RFID chips ingeniously, triggering the display of relevant videos when customers interact with specific items. For example, picking up a garment will cause to show video showing the item on a runway or detailing its manufacturing process. This interactive use of technology enhances the customer's understanding and connection to the products. Featuring entertaining touches such as meticulously timed 'digital rain showers' and a dedicated space for customers to personalize their coats, 'Burberry World Live' transcends the ordinary retail experience. The concept incorporates live streaming of Burberry fashion shows and events. Customers in the flagship stores can virtually attend and experience the latest collections as if they were present at the event. This not only enhances the in-store atmosphere but also connects customers directly with the brand's global happenings.[11]

---

[10] Vgl. Zhu, Zhengjia: "The Impact of Digital Transformation on the Fashion Industry in the Post-Pandemic Era", researchgate.com, April 2023
(https://www.researchgate.net/publication/370578695_The_Impact_of_Digital_Transformation_on_the_Fashion_Industry_in_the_Post-Pandemic_Era letzter Stand: 27.12.2023)

[11] Vgl. Ho, Lauren: "The digitally enhanced new Burberry flagship store, London", wallpaper.com, 07.10.2022)
(https://www.wallpaper.com/fashion/the-digitally-enhanced-new-burberry-flagship-store-london letzter Stand: 10.11.2023)

To further elevate the shopping experience, all store employees are equipped with iPads containing a comprehensive database of customer purchase history and preferences. This integration of technology enables the staff to provide a more personalized and unique shopping experience for each customer.[12] The store does not contain any real cashier points. The staff is accessorized with a credit card machine for transactions, making the buying process as short as possible and giving the customer almost no opportunity to have second thoughts regarding their purchase.[13]

4.3 Case study 2: The digital retail stores in China and Japan

While already having opened a digital store in London in 2012, Burberry claims the store in Shenzhen, China is their first "social retail store". With China making up to 40% of Burberry's annual sales and a constant growth in the Chinese market, the brand found it to be the optimal place to test out the concept of "social retail store". One of the main features is the use and collaboration of the app WeChat, China's foremost messaging app boasting over 1 billion users. Marco Gobbetti, Burberry's CEO at the time claims "When it came to innovating around social and retail, China was the obvious place to go as home to some of the most digitally savvy luxury customers. Together with Tencent, we have pioneered a new concept that will redefine expectations of luxury retail."

The collaboration between Burberry and Tencent-owned WeChat was meticulously thought out, focusing on how WeChat could enhance the shopping experience at Burberry, given the significant time consumers spend on the platform. Recognizing that 80% of Burberry's customers engage with digital touchpoints prior to in-person shopping, the integration with WeChat proves highly advantageous. Shoppers at Burberry can leverage a mini program to reserve fitting rooms, select items for try-on, schedule appointments with sales associates, and share exclusive content on social media. The scanning of a product's QR code using WeChat allows customers to access additional information about the merchandise available

---

[12] Vgl. S., Petey: „Burberry's Digital Transformation", harvard.edu, 18.11.2016
(https://d3.harvard.edu/platform-rctom/submission/burberrys-digital-transformation/ letzter Stand: 10.11.2023)
[13] Vgl. Ho, Lauren: "The digitally enhanced new Burberry flagship store, London", wallpaper.com, 07.10.2022
(https://www.wallpaper.com/fashion/the-digitally-enhanced-new-burberry-flagship-store-london letzter Stand: 10.11.2023)

in the store. The app also facilitates the booking of store tours and reservations at Thomas, the in-store café, providing customers with a convenient and integrated experience.[14] Customers can accumulate digital currency by participating in a game through a WeChat mini program, which can then be exchanged for rewards, including exclusive menu items at the café. The Thomas is also used to involve customers into a community space for workshops, exhibitions, and live performances.[15]

As Burberry advances its transformation strategy, it not only elevates its position further into the upmarket segment but also embraces technological innovation to distinguish itself within the realm of luxury brands. Burberry is effectively erasing the boundary between online and offline sales through strategic initiatives that seamlessly integrate digital and physical retail channels. The brand is leveraging technology to create a cohesive shopping experience for customers, ensuring a fluid transition between the online and offline realms. This approach involves the implementation of innovative features such as digital mirrors, interactive displays, and RFID technology in stores.

4.4 Burberry's Digital Transformation type

Burberry's adoption of digital technologies in its retail spaces, online platforms, and customer engagement strategies contributes to a transformation in its business model, especially in terms of how it interacts with customers and delivers products.

There is also happening a cultural transformation within the company, especially in China. Burberry created a platform and space to be social and interactive, with the WeChat app and the Thomas café connected to it. Burberry enables to connect over their luxury products through a social network and exchange opinions and ideas. By using a physical café within the store as part of their marketing and digital transformation strategy, Burberry is creating a place to incorporate unique and innovative elements into its flagship stores, creating immersive brand experiences for customers.

---

[14] Vgl. McKinnon, Tricia: "How Burberry is Building the Store of the Future", indigo9digital.com, 03.06.2022
(https://www.indigo9digital.com/blog/burberrysocialretailstoreofthefuture letzter Stand: 10.11.2023)
[15] Vgl. Halliday, Sandra: „Burberry opens virtual store with Elle Digital in Japan", fashionnetwork.com, 19.03.2021
(https://ww.fashionnetwork.com/news/Burberry-opens-virtual-store-with-elle-digital-in-japan,1288820.html letzter Stand: 10.11.2023)

Burberry's emphasis on digital technology and innovation, as seen in its flagship stores and online presence, contributes to a cultural shift toward embracing a more tech-savvy and forward-thinking mindset. Burberry's digital strategy is based on the recognition that sales channels are rapidly changing. While traditional face-to-face retail is becoming less important, Burberry understands the need to reinvent it for a luxury brand. This can be achieved through a combination of tactile experiences and digital elements. Flagship stores play a crucial role in this digital transformation. Burberry previously suffered a decline in their brand reputation two decades ago and are determined to avoid a repeat of this. A strong brand is crucial for achieving favorable profit margins and expansion.

5. Future Directions

According to Burberry's website, the brand has improved its digital brand positioning and product offerings from 2017 to 2022, reflecting its unique qualities and heritage. The brand aims to focus on revenue growth in its next phase and has a longer-term ambition of becoming a £5 billion revenue brand, with a significant increase in operating leverage and operating profit margin above 20%.[16]

The key elements of Burberry's strategy include brand image, communications, products, distribution, and enablers. In terms of digital communication, Burberry aims to deliver a consistent brand message across all touchpoints, both internationally and within all points of sale. Additionally, the company is committed to enhancing customer focus and centricity. Regarding distribution, the brand aims to accelerate store refurbishments and turn more stores into digital stores globally, not just in England and Asia. The goal is to strengthen their distribution by quickly introducing their new store concept worldwide and enhancing their presence in important global hubs. The brand also aims to strengthen its relationship with customers and the community through innovation and the creation of new digitally powered experiences. Burberry is also taking advantage of opportunities in e-commerce, enhancing the user experience across websites and mobile apps, enabling customers to better connect with the brand and discover their love for Burberry more easily.[17]

---

[16] „Strategy" burberryplc.com
(https://www.burberryplc.com/company/strategy letzter Stand: 15.01.2024)
[17] Strategy" burberryplc.com
(https://www.burberryplc.com/company/strategy letzter Stand: 15.01.2024)

The brand names execution as the key to delivering this strategy, aiming to simplify processes, and improving efficiency in their company areas such as product development and supply chain, while also ensuring a better connection between merchandising and design. Burberry also wants to positively impact their communities and create a more digitally enhanced and improved outcome for customers, employees and stakeholders.[18]

---

[18] „Strategy" burberryplc.com
(https://www.burberryplc.com/company/strategy letzter Stand: 15.01.2024)

6. Conclusion

The ongoing digital transformation and recent events such as the pandemic have led to changes in customer shopping habits, which in turn have influenced the way brands approach digitalization. Burberry has successfully integrated this strategy into its business model by using technology to connect online and offline markets for product sales and services, improving customer accessibility and communication within the brand. The brand can respond flexibly to any disruptions and is using digital technology in its physical stores to create a unique customer experience, which draws customers' attention back to physical stores. Taking Burberry as an example, the company's digital transformation should be recognized as a necessity and an opportunity to establish a digital strategy suitable for the company's direction in the digitalized and post-pandemic era.

By seamlessly merging the online shopping experience with cutting-edge digital technology, Burberry's flagship store in London not only offers unparalleled customer engagement but also solidifies the brand's position as a leader in innovative retail experiences. As the brand is embracing their digital advancements, Burberry aims to provide customers with a unified and enhanced shopping journey, reinforcing its commitment to blurring the lines between the traditional and digital retail landscapes. Burberry's integration of digital retail stores effectively enhances customer engagement. In the early 2000s, the brand underwent a crisis and required innovative solutions to reposition itself as a luxury brand. Burberry recognized the importance of selling a lifestyle rather than just a product, and successfully offered customers a progressive and innovative luxury experience.

7. Sources

Halliday, Sandra: „Burberry opens virtual store with Elle Digital in Japan", fashionnetwork.com, 19.03.2021
(https://ww.fashionnetwork.com/news/Burberry-opens-virtual-store-with-elle-digital-in-japan,1288820.html letzter Stand: 10.11.2023)

Ho, Lauren: "The digitally enhanced new Burberry flagship store, London", wallpaper.com, 07.10.2022)
(https://www.wallpaper.com/fashion/the-digitally-enhanced-new-burberry-flagship-store-london letzter Stand: 10.11.2023)

McKinnon, Tricia: "How Burberry is Building the Store of the Future", indigo9digital.com, 03.06.2022

(https://www.indigo9digital.com/blog/burberrysocialretailstoreofthefuture letzter Stand: 10.11.2023)

S., Petey: „Burberry's Digital Transformation", harvard.edu, 18.11.2016

(https://d3.harvard.edu/platform-rctom/submission/burberrys-digital-transformation/ letzter Stand: 10.11.2023)

Sacolick, Isaac: „Digital transformation challenges and 14 ways to solve them", techtarget.com, 01.11.2023

(https://www.techtarget.com/searchcio/tip/3-biggest-digital-transformation-challenges-and-how-to-solve-them letzter Stand: 14.01.2024)

Zhu, Zhengjia: "The Impact of Digital Transformation on the Fashion Industry in the Post-Pandemic Era", researchgate.com, April 2023
(https://www.researchgate.net/publication/370578695_The_Impact_of_Digital_Transformation_on_the_Fashion_Industry_in_the_Post-Pandemic_Era letzter Stand: 27.12.2023)

„Burberry: Our History", burberry.com
(https://uk.burberry.com/c/our-history/ letzter Stand: 08.11.2023)

„House History: The Burberry Timeline" hautehistory.co.uk, 28.07.2020
(http://www.hautehistory.co.uk/burberry-timeline/house-history-the-burberry-timeline letzter Stand: 08.11.2023)

Strategy" burberryplc.com

(https://www.burberryplc.com/company/strategy letzter Stand: 15.01.2024)

„Sustainable Development Goals" burberry.com

(https://www.burberryplc.com/impact/Our-Approach/sustainable-development-goals
letzter Stand: 08.11.2023)

„What is digital transformation?", Accenture.com

(https://www.accenture.com/us-en/insights/digital-transformation-index#   letzter   Stand:
14.01.2024)

YOUR KNOWLEDGE HAS VALUE